CROSS COUNTRY SKIING IN YOSEMITE

Glacier Point　　　　　*photo by Chris Falkenstein*

CROSS COUNTRY SKIING IN YOSEMITE

by
Tim Messick

CHOCKSTONE PRESS

Denver, Colorado
1985

Published by
Chockstone Press
526 Franklin Street
Denver, Colorado 80218

Printed in the United States of America

ISBN 0-9609452-4-5

Cover photo by Chris Falkenstein

ACKNOWLEDGEMENTS

In preparing this book, many people have shared advice, information, and encouragement. Without their help this guide would not be as complete or informative. Thanks to Loyd Price, Bruce Brossman and the entire Yosemite Cross Country Ski School. Special thanks to Sigrid Johanson for the excellent maps and graphs, Nanci Adinolfi, Bob Ashworth, Chris Cox, Chris Falkenstein, Bill Frey, Lewis Goldman, Dan Hancock, Wayne Merry, Dave Norris, Don Reid, Howard Weamer, and Dirk Van Winkle, for technical information and to my mom for the calligraphy, and overall to my mom and dad for encouraging me to ski and for backing my trip to Yosemite in the first place. Thanks also to the National Park Service for the use of their Winter Wilderness Use brochure, from which I borrowed heavily. Finally, I want to thank the Yosemite Winter Club for the use of the "Skier's Ten Commandments."

All uncredited photos by the author.

FOREWORD

Ski Touring: A Yosemite Tradition

Ski Touring in Yosemite is as traditional as snow in winter. The Yosemite Mountaineering School is a part of that tradition, as well as other local Yosemite ski organizations. Ski touring in Yosemite has been a major winter sport since the mid-forties. The early skiers used their wooden skis and seal-skin climbers for transportation, recreation and competition. There was no difference between an "uphill" ski and a "downhill" ski. One pair of skis was used for all types of skiing.

Skiers leaving the Badger Pass area in the early years were hearty souls and had the spirit of adventure. Now in the eighties that spirit has reached new levels. The rebirth of the skier as adventurer, explorer and seeker of the untracked slope, has brought skiers by the thousands to the Yosemite region, with over 90 miles of marked trails.

So often we cross-country skiers hear comments by uneducated alpine skiers, like: "How can that be fun, all you do is ski on flat terrain?" or "It looks like so much work." All these folks have to do to taste what cross-country can be is to take a spin to Dewey Point or some other trail with exciting downhill runs and great views. Soon these skeptical alpine skiers will return to the basics of skiing and will be more aware of the delicate balance common to both alpine and cross-country skiing. Quickly enough they will see how much fun this old sport of ski touring can bring them.

Major innovations have certainly helped the return of skis as multi-functional tools. Waxless skis probably have had more to do with getting people on cross-country skis than any other innovation. They enable the "casual tourer" to put on skis and go, with only having to prepare the skis for easier gliding (i.e. Maxi Glide or glide wax wiped on the bottoms).

Learning to apply wax on waxable skis is an added challenge. Waxing in the Sierra is nearly an art form. Several layers of wax and klisters are often used, sometimes making the bottoms look like a Jackson Pollack painting. A well waxed ski will out perform any waxless model. They are faster, more responsive and grip better in all conditions. Of course, this is dependent upon the right wax combination being chosen.

As a first pair of skis, a waxless version is recommended. This is due to their simplicity in use and care. With so many brands and types of skis, boots, poles and bindings on the market today, the novice can be quickly confused about what to choose. To avoid confusion go to a professional school and rental shop, and take a lesson using their equipment. This helps to insure a good first experience on cross-country skis, which is critical to future enjoyment of the sport.

Soon you'll be able to deal with whatever the cross-country trail throws at you. A common trail has hills, dips, bumps, trees and many other fun challenges. Enjoyment will increase as you learn to control your skis on the terrain changes you encounter.

In time, Dewey Point, Glacier Point, the Ghost Forest loop and most any trail will become skiable and fun. Whether you choose citizen racing, day touring, overnighters, down-skiing or ski-mountaineering, you'll surely feel as other skiers do: Cross-country skiing is very rewarding. The exercise, thrilling views and solitude experienced will certainly keep you coming back. Yosemite, with its well marked trails, groomed tracks, beautiful backcountry and Badger Pass for practicing your turns is certainly a place to come back to.

Tim Messick learned to ski in Virginia as a teenager, and has done all types of skiing in Yosemite for over five years. He has taught lessons and guided many backcountry trips for the Yosemite Mountaineering School. He has written an invitation to new adventures, but enjoy the Yosemite winter with proper preparation, caution and common sense. Combining all this, have a safe Yosemite winter experience. We'll see you on the trails.

Bruce Brossman

Director, Yosemite Cross Country Ski School

CONTENTS

Above the Snow Creek switchbacks

TOURS IN YOSEMITE

Day tours in Yosemite are numerous, yet they are all different. Some will take a full day to complete, while others will take only a few hours. Some tours take you high on ridges and steal your heart with views of some of the most breath-taking scenery on earth, while others follow along streams, through red fir or lodgepole pine forests, offering quiet solitude with every stride. A day tour in Yosemite can mean a quick jaunt to Dewey Point and back wearing shorts and a T-shirt on a 65 degree "bluebird" day, to a narrow escape with an avalanche in horrendous winds and snow on Illilouette Ridge in February.

Cross country skiing in Yosemite centers around three areas of the Park. Many trails lead out of the Badger Pass Ski Area, an alpine skiing resort located several miles south of, but 3200 feet above, Yosemite Valley. These trails lead to high meadows and lakes in the backcountry of the Park, and to view points that overlook the Valley, including the famous Glacier Point. Another focal point of cross country skiing is centered around Crane Flat, a high forested area located sixteen miles to the northwest of Yosemite Valley. For more experienced skiers, much skiing is done out of a base camp located in Tuolumne Meadows, that wonderful highcountry area twenty miles to the east of Yosemite Valley. The road to Tuolumne is not plowed in the winter, leaving the exquisite pleasures of the area reserved for those with skis.

A special feature of some trails in the Badger Pass area is the use of a machine to groom and set tracks for cross country skiers. The snow on the road is groomed by machine, and a "double track-setter" sled, attached behind, sets beautifully skiable tracks, similar in quality and looks to those tracks set by a pair of skiers. The tracks start from the Badger Pass Ski Area and go to Glacier Point by way of the unplowed Glacier Point Road, a round-trip distance of twenty miles. There is also a mile long loop of machine-set tracks in the Bridalveil Creek Campground, adjacent to the Glacier Point Road.

Machine setting of tracks was first tested in Yosemite during the winter of 1982-'83. Most of the tracks set at that time were a result of having to send a snow machine to Glacier Point for emergency maintenance on buildings and electrical equipment. A home-made wooden track sled was attached with a rope to the snow machine and pulled behind, making crude but skiable tracks. The tracks now set by machine make Nordic skiing safer, easier to learn, and give beginning skiers easier access to Yosemite's backcountry. Without a doubt, the new tracks and trailhead have helped change ski touring in Yosemite for the better.

Ski tracks on all the other trails are left to be "set" by the first skiers on the trail after a new snowfall. Skiers breaking a new trail are rewarded with a sense of being in the wilderness that is not always found while following someone else's tracks. Although skier-made tracks are not as consistent in quality as those set by machine, it is sometimes difficult to tell the difference.

HOW TO USE THIS BOOK

Trailhead signs at the start of most trails indicate the particular trail number, mileage, direction of travel, and estimated time of travel. Bright yellow, triangular markers are nailed to the trees along the trail, showing the route. The markers show changes in direction and remaining mileage. Most of the markers are made of reflective material and are visible at night with a flashlight. However, without a full moon, night skiing is not recommended. Exact mileage on these trails is difficult to ascertain, as is evidenced by a number of contradictions seen on the trail signs throughout the Park. Because this book strives to be accurate in its mileage references, distances given here, while approximations, may vary from mileages seen on trail signs.

A quality rating system is used with each description in the book. Three stars is the highest quality; no Yosemite trail deserves less than one star. The quality rating is based on the esthetics of a given tour. Streams, exciting downhill runs, groves of trees, rock bands and scenic views all influence the star quality system. All ski tours in Yosemite are very special and only a trail with thick, dense forest, difficult conditions or poor trail markers deserves a one star rating.

Difficulty signs are the same as those used in Alpine Skiing. The green circle means "easiest", the blue square "more difficult" and the black diamond "most difficult". Keep in mind that these ratings will vary depending on snow conditions.

The time needed to ski a given trail may vary greatly, depending on the skier. One person may take one hour to ski a trail that another skis in five. "Average ski times" are simply a conservative estimate of how long it may take an "average intermediate skier" to cover a certain trail. Faster, more experienced skiers can estimate their time by consulting the elevation graph and checking mileage and difficulty ratings before starting out.

WINTER WILDERNESS USE RULES

— Camp out of sight of any marked ski trail, including all unplowed roads.
— Camp at least 100' from any water source, drainage, or summer use area.

— No camping is allowed within one mile of any plowed road.

— Crane Flat, Summit Meadow, Peregoy Meadow, and all Big Trees groves are day use areas and closed to camping. Exception: Upper Grove of Mariposa Big Trees is open to camping.

— All overnight ski trips require a Wilderness Permit from the National Park Service. They are available free of charge at the Yosemite Valley Visitor's Center or at the Ranger "A Frame" building at the Badger Pass Ski Area. They are open between 8-5:00 pm.

— Pets are not permitted beyond plowed roads.

— Oversnow vehicles are not permitted.

— All trash must be packed out.

— Snowshoers using marked trails should stay four feet from ski track.

— The cutting of tree limbs or boughs is prohibited.

— Washing in streams or open bodies of water is not permitted. Protect water quality by proper human waste disposal and disposal of rinse/wash water at least 100' from camp area or water sources. All drinking water taken from open sources should be purified by boiling vigorously for at least one minute, or by chemical treatment with iodine based purifier. Cold water must be treated for at least twice the recommended time.

BACK COUNTRY COURTESIES

With the increasing numbers of cross-country skiers, a few common courtesies should help things go a little smoother on the trail.

— When stopping to make adjustments on equipment or clothing, step off to the side of the tracks to avoid possible collisions from other skiers.

— Always give the downhill skier the right of way. It is usually easier for the person going uphill to step out of the track first.

— Breaking trail in new snow is often difficult, but the tracks that you set will be used by other skiers, so try to make them a "work of art", by making them as straight and even as possible.

— Try to ski in the right-hand track when there are more than one set of tracks.

— When passing another skier, care should be made not to tangle each others poles.

SAFETY CONSIDERATIONS

— Let someone know your plans and when you are due back.

— Be prepared for the weather; have storm gear, sunglasses and sunscreen.

— Carry map and compass; stay oriented.

— Do not separate from your group.

— Choose a reasonable goal and don't overextend yourself; know your limits. Don't start your ski trip late in the day. The snow is usually easier to ski in the morning, and getting caught in the darkness is no fun.

— Carry a whistle and signal mirror.
— Carry enough emergency equipment to spend a night out if necessary.
— Beware of hypothermia; know its symptoms and treatment.
— Beware of avalanches.
— Always practice minimum impact.
— Eat lots, and carry extra food to nibble all day.
— Drink lots. You need a gallon of fluids a day during strenuous winter activity (not alcohol!).
— Power lines in the Glacier Point area are charged with high voltage electricity during the winter. If skiing off the trail, be alert of the lines.
—Watch for signs of storm, and check the weather forecast before setting out on your trip.
—In the event of an accident, notify a Park Ranger as soon as possible. Request first aid, if available, from a qualified person such as a Nordic Ski Instructor, or one of the Nordic Park Rangers.

MINIMUM IMPACT WILDERNESS USE
Leave no trace of your visit to the wilderness—please follow these guidelines when camping.
— Camp out of sight of all trails or any summer use area.
— The use of stoves is encouraged. Open fires should be used only in emergency situations.
— Make no campsite improvements by cutting boughs etc.
— Pack out all trash.
— Human waste is a serious problem in winter. Minimize the health hazard by using a proper location if a restroom is not available. Use the "well" or indentation around a tree trunk, and dig down to soil if possible for burial of solid wastes. Be sure you are not in or near an area used in summer or near any sort of water source or drainage. Burn toilet paper. Backcountry restrooms are available at Summit Meadow, Bridalveil Campground and Glacier Point. Please use them.

CLOTHING
Clothing plays a big role in how comfortable you will be on your ski tour. Loose fitting clothing is recommended which can be taken on or off as the day's weather dictates. Wool or stretch nylon knickers work well in conjunction with wool socks, wool hat and gloves, polypropylene underwear, a light jacket or insulated vest, and an outer shell of wind-proof garments. For stormy days some type of waterproof rain-gear is in order. You should be able to maintain a comfortable body temperature when the air is between 10 and 65 degrees Fahrenheit. It is important to be prepared for any conditions that might arise. The weather can change fast. Don't judge how nice a day might be by the clear, blue sky of a morning.

Extra socks made from wool or polypropelene are light insurance against unexpected wet and cold hands or feet. Long underwear is a must for really cold days. Turtleneck shirts keep the critical neck area warm. Sunglasses and sunscreen are essential protection against the glare of the sun; for extra protection a visor is helpful. Gaiters that cover the boots and go up to just below the knee help keep feet and legs warmer and dryer.

EQUIPMENT

The equipment that a skier uses should be appropriate to his or her measurements. Borrowing cousin Henry's equipment for Ruby's little sister probably won't do. Having the proper gear can make a big difference in the amount of fun you'll have. Take time to buy or rent the correct equipment from a knowledgeable staff.

In the scope of cross-country skiing in Yosemite, many different types of gear can be used. By choosing the type of equipment for the type of skiing that you want to do, a lot of problems can be avoided.

If backcountry skiing is what you are after, choose a sturdy ski with metal edges, a stiff boot with lug soles, sturdy aluminum poles, and bindings that are able to withstand the rigors of backcountry skiing. A lightweight shovel is essential for safe backcountry travel in possible avalanche areas.

Climbing skins made from synthetic material permit the ski some forward glide, yet will grip when downward pressure is applied, preventing the skis from slipping back. They are fastened to the base of the ski with a special adhesive that allows easy removal for smooth, waxfree downhill skiing. The use of skins enable skiers going up hills to expend less energy, and without having to stop to wax, allow faster times. When skiing downhill with a heavy pack the use of skins can help skiers control their speed. Carrying and using climbing skins is recommended for all back-country travel, particularly by those new to winter overnight trips.

For skiing mostly in tracks, and some off-track skiing, choose a general waxable or waxless ski with a sturdy medium weight boot, pole, binding combination. Citizen racing and skiing on prepared tracks requires a lightweight outfit of waxable or waxless skis with high quality boots poles and bindings. They are more comfortable and perform more efficiently in groomed, set tracks. Track skis do not work well in the back country.

A sleeping bag rated to at least zero is recommended, as temperatures regularly dip to single digits or below throughout the ski season. Down bags, light and warm, will loose their insulating value when they get wet. Synthetic fiber-filled bags, while retaining their warmth when wet, are bulkier than down to pack. An insulating sleeping pad is needed between your sleeping bag and tent floor. A full length pad is recommended for maximum comfort. Closed cell foam pads provide warmth and does not soak up moisture. Other more comfortable and expensive pads are available.

Repair items should be carried on all ski trips. A screwdriver, duct tape, wire, knife, extra binding, spare ski tip, and hose clamps provide a relatively light but useful kit.

A basic first aid kit and knowledge of first aid fundamentals should also accompany every trip.

Crossing Olmstead Point   *photo by Chris Cox*

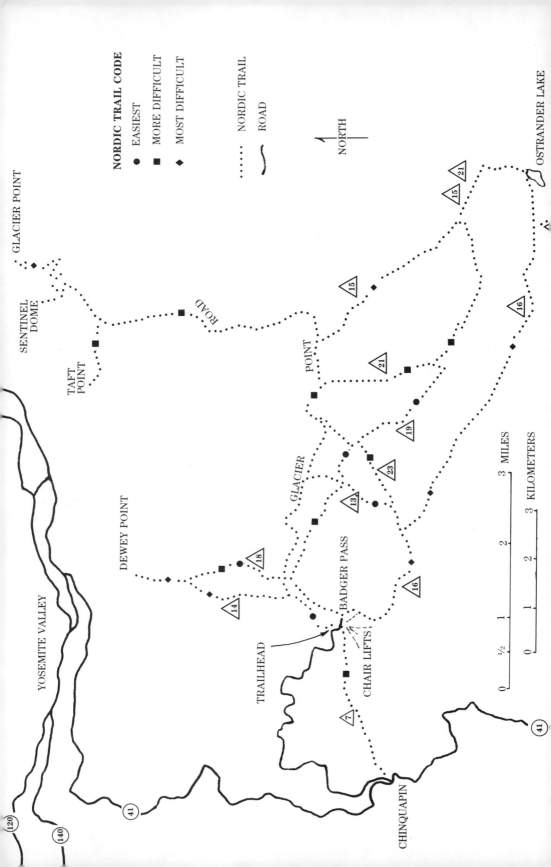

BADGER PASS AREA

Badger Pass is a place that skiers of all kinds can enjoy. The downhill ski area is mellow in a low-key family way. An excellent area to learn to downhill ski, Badger Pass is the oldest continuously operating ski area in California. The Yosemite Cross Country Ski School, fourteen years in business and now based at Badger Pass, has seen it's share of the action as well. It is no surprise that ski film maker Warren Miller has used cross-country footage shot near Badger for one of his most impressive ski films, "Snowonder".

With the new trailhead and the advent of machine-set ski tracks to Glacier Point, cross country skiing is better than ever in the Badger Pass area. The closeness of the downhill slopes to the set tracks gives skiers access to some of the best terrain anywhere to practice all aspects of cross country skiing.

After a morning of skiing the trails, why not have lunch on the sundeck at the downhill ski area. Then at 1 o'clock buy a half-day lift ticket, and spend the rest of the afternoon "gravity skiing", letting the mechanized lifts get you up the hill while the only thing you'll have to lift is your heel, to telemark down.

Whichever type of skiing you choose to do at Badger Pass, you can call ahead for the latest road, weather and avalanche conditions. For road and weather conditions call (209) 372-4605. For current slope conditions call (209) 372-1330.

Many trails described for the area start from the unplowed Glacier Point Road at various distances from the main parking lot. The mileage given for each trail is from the Glacier Point trailhead at Badger Pass.

Parking for the Glacier Point trailhead is easily reached just after turning into the Badger Pass Ski Area. Take the first left into the parking lot. The trailhead is at the top of the knoll on the left. The machine-set tracks usually start here.

CONTOUR INTERVAL 80 FEET

GLACIER POINT TRAILHEAD
TO SUMMIT MEADOW

★★★   **Quality Rating**
●   **Easiest**
1.0 mile each way
Average Skier Time: 30 minutes each way

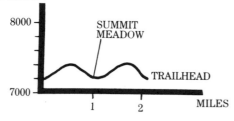

Once on the Glacier Point Road, a gradual uphill ski passes Trail #14 on the left. The road goes easily downhill to Summit Meadow, on the right. Located here are backcountry toilets and picnic tables, although they are sometimes covered with snow.

Summit Meadow is an excellent place for beginning and intermediate skiers. It has terrain to please anyone, and snow conditions are good most of the time.For beginners Summit Meadow is an ideal spot to practice the basics of cross country skiing. It is an easy goal for most skiers and makes a nice first ski tour.

Dewey Point trailhead #18, enters on the left near the far end of the meadow.

DEWEY POINT TRAIL #18

★★★   **Quality Rating**
♦   **Most Difficult**
4 miles each way
Average Skier Time: 3 hours each way

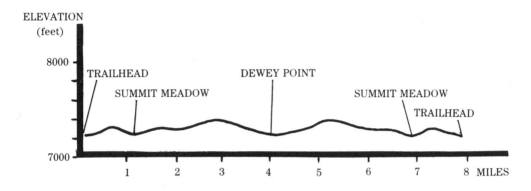

To reach the Dewey Point trail, ski one mile down the Glacier Point Road to Summit Meadow from the trailhead at the Badger Pass Ski Area. This classic tour is rated "most difficult" because of the hilly sections toward the rim of Yosemite Valley. The first half of the trail, however, has some excellent beginners' terrain. At the far end of Summit Meadow, turn left at the Dewey Point Trailhead #18. Follow the yellow trail markers through the beautiful red fir and lodgepole pine forests into Dewey Meadow. Ski through the right side of the meadow, funneling into the woods and rising up "Carolyn's Hill", a great spot for practicing turns. Continue on fairly level ground to the junction of Trails #14 and #18. This is a good turnaround point for the less experienced skier, not ready to tackle the hills ahead. From this junction on to Dewey Point the terrain is more challenging. Follow trail markers #14 and #18 one more mile to Dewey Point. Use caution here as it is a long way to the Valley floor, and the trip would be your last! The views are unique and breathtaking toward Yosemite Valley and Tuolumne Meadows and east to the Cathedral and Clark ranges. El Capitan is directly across the Valley, with the Cathedral Rocks and Spires just below. On a clear day the Coastal Range can be seen rising out of the central valley fog, 150 miles to the west.For an interesting loop ski back via Trail #14.

DEWEY POINT VIA TRAIL #14

★★ **Quality Rating**
♦ **Most Difficult**
3.75 miles each way
Average Skier Time: 2.5 hours each way

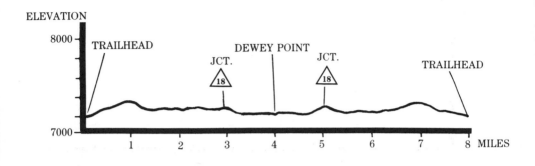

Dewey Point Trail #14 starts ¾ mile from the parking area at Badger Pass, thus providing a stretch of machine set track to warm up on before attempting the tricky Dewey Point Trail. Trail #14 is a less popular and a bit more difficult route to Dewey Point than Trail #18. Open areas along the way not only provide nice views, but offer pleasant terrain to ski as well. Trail #14 leaves the Glacier Point Road from the top of a knoll, just before Summit Meadow. Follow the markers, traversing at first, before taking a turn up the hill. Level off, then drop down some hills and over a snowy roller coaster before connecting with Trail #18, about a mile ahead of Dewey Point. Trail #14 is not frequently travelled, so don't expect to already have tracks to ski in. This is a good route for practicing with your map and compass, and for practicing your turns.

OLD GLACIER POINT ROAD TO BRIDALVEIL CREEK CAMPGROUND

★★ **Quality Rating**
■ **More Difficult**
3 miles each way
Average Skier Time: 2 hours each way

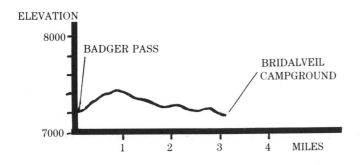

The Old Glacier Point Road begins at the Badger Pass Ski Area near the base of the "Rabbit" run. Ascend the snowcat track about ½ mile to where the old road diverges to the left.Take this and travel on mostly level terrain, passing a trail that leads left to Summit Meadow and the new Glacier Point Road.Continuing on the old road, meander through the forest on gentle terrain. The trail gradually begins to drop in elevation, providing a good, challenging downhill run. Be aware that in wet, low-snow winters, creeks cut across the trail, and it can be very difficult to cross them without taking off your skis. The Limit trail intersects at the bottom of the hill. From here Westfall Meadow is to the south and Peregoy Meadow is to the north. The Bridalveil Campground Road is reached about three miles from the start. The new Glacier Point Road is to the left ½ mile and the Ghost Forest Loop Trail is straight ahead.

LIMIT TRAIL LOOP
TRAILS #13 and #16

★★   **Quality Rating**
◆   **Most Difficult**
7.5 miles round trip
Average Skier Time: 7 hours round trip

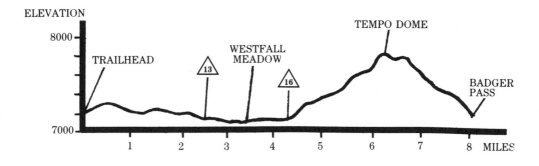

After skiing 2½ miles on the Old Glacier Point Road from Badger Pass, you'll intersect the Limit Trail. (See the previous tour.) From the Limit Trail-Old Glacier Point Road junction, turn right and head for Westfall Meadow via Trail #13. Ski along the rolling terrain, up and over the ridge to Westfall Meadow. Here Trail #23 travels along the east side of the meadow, looping back and connecting to the Bridalveil Campground road. Trail #13 continues across Westfall Meadow to the right, and follows up and around to a junction with Trail #16. Ski uphill on Trail #16 through thick forest and manzanita, eventually to the top of panoramic Tempo Dome. Fabulous views of the high country may be seen from here. Ski down the west side of Tempo Dome, following trail markers that lead to the top of "Eagle" run, at Badger Pass. Choose a run down that suits your ability. "Rabbit" or "Beaver" runs are the easiest, and usually not as crowded as the others. If you can ski this loop feeling good and confident at the end, you should be able to ski most any trail in the area without too much difficulty. Reversing the route, starting at the top of "Eagle" run and returning via the old or new Glacier Point road provides a nice alternate to this trip.

Yosemite Valley skiers   *photo by Chris Cox*

BRIDALVEIL MEADOW-GHOST FOREST LOOP #19

★   **Quality Rating**
■   **More Difficult**
Miles: 13 round trip
Average Skier Time: 8 hours round trip

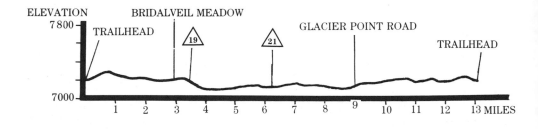

Bridalveil Meadow lies just off the new Glacier Point Road, three miles east of Badger Pass, and is also bordered by the Bridalveil Campground Road. Trail #19 starts from a trailhead sign at the north end of the meadow. Follow along the left side of the meadow, skiing fairly close to, and across Bridalveil Creek. The markers continue through thick stands of lodgepole pines. Needle-miner-moths have killed many of the trees; the moth larvae eat the pine needles from the inside out, causing them to eventually turn brown and die. This is where the term "ghost forest" originated. The Bridalveil Creek Trail (#21) eventually joins Trail #19. Ski back via Trail #21 to the Glacier Point Road, thus making a long, but not too difficult loop to Badger Pass. The Ghost Forest Trail is also a good way to link up with the Bridalveil Creek Trail to Ostrander Lake. This trail provides the shortest, and usually easiest way to Ostrander Lake. Be aware that in places the trail goes through very thick lodgepole pine stands, and a large backpack could catch a lot of snags. After a new snowfall trail markers might be blocked from vision, and the trail-breaking can be difficult through the dense timber.

CHINQUAPIN SKI TRAIL (#7)

★★★   **Quality Rating**
■   **More Difficult**
2.7 miles one way
Average Skier Time: 45 minutes

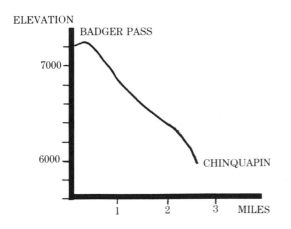

This trail drops from the downhill area at Badger to the Chinquapin restroom parking lot, on Highway 41 at the turnoff to Badger Pass. With 1300 feet of elevation loss, it is an exciting downhill run on touring gear, and a great finish to your day of skiing. Pick up the #7 trail markers about one third of the way up the 'Bruin' run, on the right side of the ski area as you face the slope. Follow the gradual downhill traverse, negotiating occasional logs, streams, and straight steep sections. The steepest part of the trail is near the end. Thick manzanita may be encountered just before the parking lot is reached. This trail is part of the Old Glacier Point Road, and in years of deep snow provides excellent skiing. Watch your speed on this one, or the inevitable surprises may be bigger than you might like. If you arrange to be picked up at the end of the trail, the occasionally hectic traffic between Badger and Highway 41 can be avoided.

BADGER PASS TO GLACIER POINT

★★★   **Quality Rating**
■ **More Difficult**
10 miles each way
Average Skier Time: 10+ hours round trip

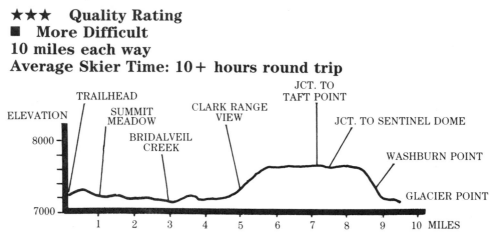

Skiing the machine set tracks to Glacier Point is becoming a popular undertaking, though one that should not be taken lightly. While strong intermediate skiers can make it to Glacier Point and back to Badger Pass in eight hours or less in prime snow conditions, few do so and enjoy any of the interesting side trips possible along the way. Skiers should be prepared for the possibility of a night out.Camping at Glacier Point is a popular alternative to a very long day of skiing.

The first 4½ miles of the road are mostly downhill skiing and the machine set tracks on this section allow smooth, exciting skiing. The road turns uphill as you reach the Trail #21 junction. After the uphill section, the road levels off and passes the Mono Meadow summer trail, on the right. Start gaining elevation once again, and enjoy views toward the southeast and the Clark Range.The road steepens as you approach the Ostrander Rocks area, with Mt. Starr King and the Clark Range now clearly visible. Along this hillside are several good lunch spots. Once at the top of the hill ski down slightly through a nicely shaded section. Pothole Meadow appears on the left and the mile long trail to the rim via the Taft Point Trail starts shortly thereafter.

Sentinel Dome soon pops up like a huge, snowy, granite balloon. The road climbs gradually and then levels off, passing the smaller domes below Sentinel, and, on the right, Illilouette Ridge. The road continues, winding around to the left, and before it begins to drop down, an obvious trail becomes visible, which leads left to Sentinel Dome.

This side trail traverses up to the east ridge, on the right. From here you can ski or walk to the top of the dome. The jeffery pine on top of the dome, first made famous by Ansel Adams, is dead now, but it still provides an excellent focal point for your photography. The snow covered wall and granite domes in the background add to the excitement of this worthwhile two mile side trip. Skiing back down the dome can be very exciting but it requires skill. The novice skier should consider walking down the ridgeline. More experienced skiers can enjoy some difficult, but nice runs down the face to the left of the walkup ridge. Conditions will vary, so scout the slope before heading down.

Once back on the Glacier Point Road it is all downhill to Washburn and Glacier Points. When the conditions are icy, the skiing here is very fast and extreme caution should be maintained. At times the trail turns quickly and unexpectedly. There is an incredible view at Washburn Point. Half Dome divides Tenaya and Merced canyons, with the high country spread out above. From Washburn Point, continue down the road past some tight turns and drop down to the saddle immediately below Glacier Point. Walk or ski up past the Yosemite Mountaineering School hut and the Geological Exhibit Shelter. Be careful here; sometimes the guard rail is snowed over and it can be difficult to determine where the edge of the cliff is. The view from Glacier Point is tremendous. In the winter, it takes on new meaning because if you started at Badger Pass, you've just skied ten difficult miles to get there. The snow-covered landscape evokes the feeling of wilderness. As the sun sets the temperature drops considerably, a reminder of the glaciers that once covered Yosemite millions of years ago. Had one been at Glacier Point during the last ice age it might have been possible to ski across the glacier to the other side of Yosemite Valley. Today we can plainly see the results of the glaciers, and appreciate the wealth of water, rocks and sun which make up this exciting view.

There are numerous campsites in the area of Glacier Point, as well as several places to create shelters of snow. Backcountry toilets are maintained there for proper sanitation.

The Yosemite Cross Country Ski School guides trips to their well-stocked hut at Glacier Point several times each month during the winter, offering a casual and comfortable backcountry experience.

Snow camping below Horse Ridge

SKIING TO THE OSTRANDER HUT

The Ostrander Ski Hut is one of those very special places in the Park where the winter visitor is able to experience the backcountry with the warmth and security of a bunkbed. Located ten miles southeast from Badger Pass, the hut is maintained by the Yosemite Natural History Association in cooperation with the National Park Service. The current cost is $6.00 per night and reservations should be made well in advance. The Yosemite Natural History Association office is located in Yosemite Valley, near the Visitor Center. The telephone number for hut reservations is (209) 372-4532. The address is P.O. Box 545, Yosemite National Park, CA 95389.

Caretakers stationed at the hut from December to April are helpful with advice and suggestions about the area. The bowls above Ostrander Lake provide some of the best skiing in Yosemite.The mostly northern exposure holds good powder, and the views are spectacular.Don't forget your gaiters!

The Yosemite Natural History Association and the Yosemite Winter Club both conduct guided tours to the hut several times each winter. For further information contact these organizations directly

Novice skiers often have a difficult, if not impossible time making it to the hut in one day. An early morning start is strongly recommended and the use of climbing skins can help prevent an unscheduled night out that could have serious consequences.

Nice day tours can be done from the hut by following the Hart Lake Trail, cutting up to the ridge that goes up to the top of Horse Ridge, and around the south side, back to Trail #16 and the hut. Touring alone in this area is not recommended because avalanche danger and hidden cliff bands are common. Play it safe and ski with a partner.

OSTRANDER LAKE VIA THE BRIDALVEIL CREEK TRAIL

★★★ **Quality Rating**
■ **More Difficult**
10 miles each way
Average Skier Time: 5-8 hours each way

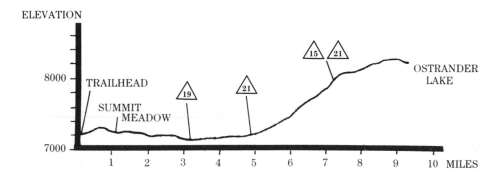

The Bridalveil Creek Trail (Trail #21) starts about four miles down the Glacier Point Road from Badger Pass.Turn right at the trailhead sign for Trail #21. This trail is an excellent choice when good, skied-in tracks have been set. The trail proceeds through mostly forested terrain along an old road bed. Many years ago this road was used to transport skiers and supplies to the hut ... ah, the good old days! The roadbed still makes the mellowest route to the hut and lake area.

Now on Trail #21, ski level to uphill for several miles. The trail reaches an opening where Trails #21 and #19 converge. Follow the markers for #21 up the hill to the intersection of Trail #15. Some call this next steep, continuous section of the trail "Heart Attack Hill." Take time to catch your breath and take in the views of Yosemite's high country. The trail continues climbing a bit more before dropping slightly to the beautiful snow covered lake and ski hut.

Glacier Point   *photo by Chris Falkenstein*

OSTRANDER LAKE VIA TRAIL #15 AND HORIZON RIDGE

★★★   **Quality Rating**
◆   **Most Difficult**
10 miles one way
Average Skier Time: 6-10 hours one way

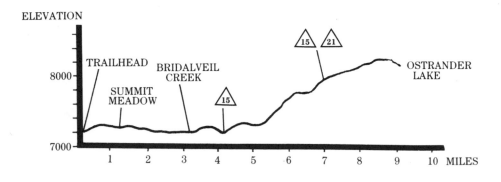

This scenic trail offers a higher, more difficult route to Ostrander Lake.This route usually has better snow coverage than the Bridalveil Creek Trail. Climbing skins are strongly recommended on this steep uphill trail. After about 4½ miles on the Glacier Point Road, you will reach the Horizon Ridge Trailhead (#15), on the right. Ski uphill through bands of forests and meadows.Occasionally a small creek or two may have to be crossed. Previous experience with log and stream crossings is helpful on this route.Gaining altitude over rolling terrain, continue nearly to the top of Horizon Ridge. There are some nice places to camp in this area. This long ridge is strenuous, especially with a heavy pack. Conserving energy here is important, as "Heart Attack Hill" lies ahead on the final climb to the hut. Trail #15 joins #21 just before this final strenuous 1½ to the hut. Soon you will be smelling smoke from the woodstove at the hut, letting you know that your long day's journey is nearly over. Less experienced parties should consider taking an extra day to ski in, especially if bad weather is imminent. The difficult terrain, combined with the cold and altitude, can make this trip seem difficult to the novice skier. The extra 300 feet of elevation gain seems enormous compared to the Bridalveil Creek Trail. Be well prepared for this one, whether you are staying at the hut or snow camping for the night.

OSTRANDER LAKE VIA
THE MERCED CREST TRAIL

★★★   **Quality Rating**
◆   **Most Difficult**
9 miles each way
Average Skier Time: 6-10 hours each way

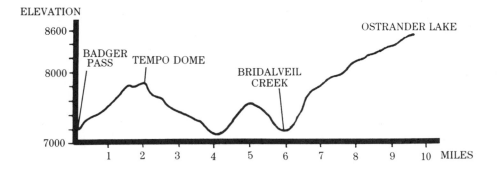

This is an exciting tour that begins at the top of "Eagle" run at the Badger Pass Ski Area. The snow cat track in front of the lodge leads to the top of Eagle run after about a mile of winding uphill terrain. Of all the trails to Ostrander Lake, this is the most continuously difficult.From the trailhead at the top of "Eagle", follow the trail markers for Trail #16 down toward Tempo Dome. Traverse right around the dome, keeping the trail markers in sight. After traversing right, the trail drops down through a mostly forested area. Reach the junction of Trail #13 and continue on #16 through some very hilly terrain. The trail then follows a series of smaller domes, the tops of which make great vantage points. Horse Ridge (above Ostrander Lake) can be seen from here. Just before Horse Ridge, the trail traverses near a smaller ridge. Avalanche danger may be very high here at certain times. Common sense should be used in determining how close a skier should traverse to this ridge. In between these two ridges is another trail intersection. Trail #16 turns left, heading toward the lake and the ski hut. Trail #17 continues up between the two ridges to the south side of Horse Ridge. The trail markers pass close to Buena Vista Peak and end after a few miles.

28

Yosemite Valley   *photo by Chris Cox*

YOSEMITE VALLEY

Cold, snowy winters sometimes lay a blanket of snow on the Valley floor. On these rare occasions the area takes on an unforgettable look. Ice rimmed waterfalls, the sounds of avalanches echoing through the canyons, and the frosty nip in the air add to the excitement of such a special place. It generally takes about a foot of snow to be able to ski in the Valley without thrashing the bottoms of your skis. Snow hikers also use these trails and therefore prime conditions will be found in the early morning hours, before the snow gets "post-holed" by the hikers.

With a couple feet of snow the possibilities of skiing in the Valley are almost inexhaustible. The many open meadows from Curry Village to Bridalveil Falls offer pristine views and easy skiing. The horse trails and footpaths may require a bit more experience to ski, but they in no way can be considered difficult. The only "hilly" areas in the Valley are located on the way to Mirror Lake. A good practice hill lies across from the stables, between the shuttle bus path and the Merced River. Years ago, before the development of Badger Pass Ski Area, this hill was used by some of Yosemite's earliest skiers. From this hill it is nearly a mile up the road to Mirror Lake. The road is level at first, but it then rises up the ten percent grade to the top of the hill and to the lake. With enough snow a loop can be skied all the way around Mirror Lake by way of horse trails. Since good skiing in the Valley is rarely possible, there is no need to describe in detail the various paths to take. It is sufficient to say that if you find yourself in the Yosemite Valley with skiable snow try to take advantage of it. Ski anywhere on the Valley floor and you can't go wrong. Just keep your distance from the base of the rock walls in case of falling ice, rock and snow. A tour around one of the meadows on a clear night with a full moon will leave a lasting impression. Huge trees, backlit by the moon, shimmering cliffs and waterfalls and an illuminated snow will invigorate your senses.

Giant Sequoias   *photo by Chris Cox*

CRANE FLAT AREA

The Crane Flat cross country ski trails lie near the junction of Highway 120 West and Highway 120 East (Tioga Pass Road), sixteen miles west of Yosemite Valley and thirty-nine miles west of Tuolumne Meadows. There are no facilities open in the winter at Crane Flat, but there is a lot of nice skiing. As the elevation is about 6,200 feet, Crane Flat gets somewhat less snow cover than the Badger Pass or Tuolumne Meadows areas, but it is still an excellent place for ski touring. The road over Tioga Pass is usually closed from mid November to the first part of May, due to snow cover. Parking and backcountry toilets are available both at the closed gas station, and the main trailhead at the end of the plowed road on Highway 120 East.

Beginning skiers, as well as those more advanced, will find trails in this area to enjoy. As the name implies, much of the surrounding area is flat, with tours that go through beautiful forests and wide open meadows. Some of the area trails, however, reach high ridges that offer great views of the surrounding country. Crane Flat tends to be less crowded than the Badger Pass area, and has a quiet beauty that makes this a special section of the Park.

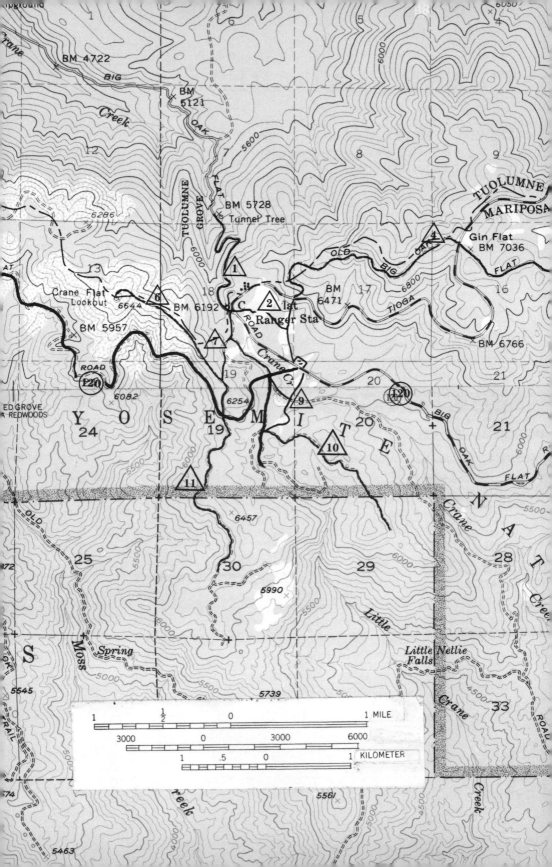

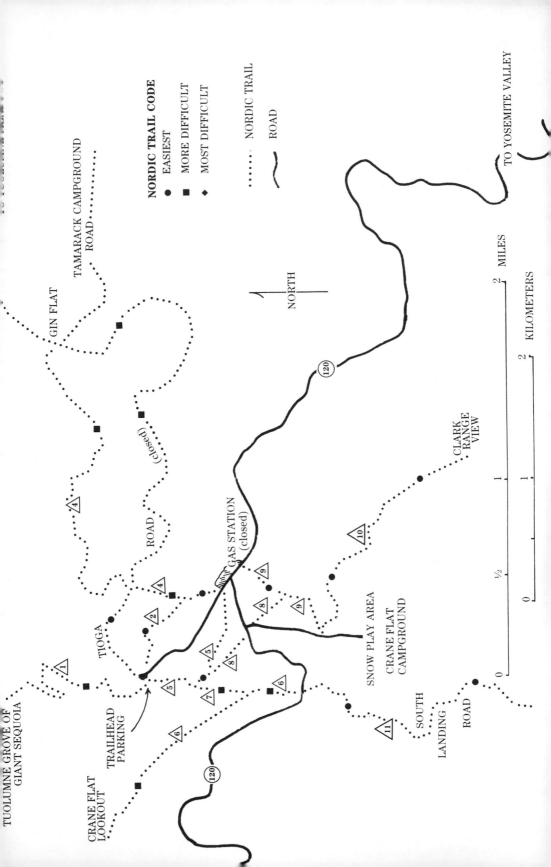

TUOLUMNE GROVE OF THE GIANT SEQUOIAS

★ **Quality Rating**
■ **More Difficult**
1.5 miles each way
Average Skier Time: 3 hours round trip

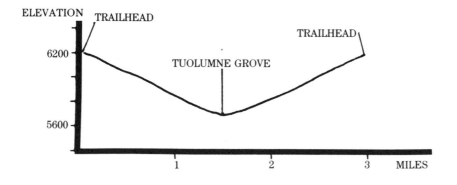

Begin this tour at the trailhead parking lot just before the closure gate on the Tioga Road. The short but steep Old Big Oak Flat Road takes you down to an inspiring grove of nature's largest living trees. The steepness of the tour is challenging and concentrating on skiing is difficult with the distraction of these grand trees at every turn. These living giants often seem all the more impressive in the winter, when the off-season visitor can usually admire their quiet dignity with solitude. The 500 feet of elevation to be gained going back up the hill is tiring, but the trip allows a longer chance to appreciate scenery that was missed on the speedy trip in. Due to the lower elevation of this trail, snow conditions tend to be icy in the mornings and slushy in the afternoons. It is only because of these difficult snow conditions that the trail is not given a higher quality rating.

CRANE FLAT MEADOW LOOP

★ **Quality Rating**
● **Easiest**
1.5 miles each way
Average Skier Time: 1 to 2 hours round trip

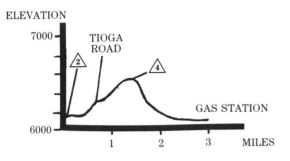

Starting at the meadow adjacent to the gas station, ski out into the middle, looking for trail marker #2. Follow the markers through the woods (to the northwest) over mostly level terrain. The occasional bumps and dips are caused by fallen trees, and their size or presence can vary from winter to winter. Continue along, gradually skiing down to Crane Flat Meadow. This meadow is large enough to hold a sizable number of skiers, and is a good place for working on technique. There are hills, flat spots and nice places to have lunch. To head back to the gas station, ski up the meadow to the east, where the snow-covered Tioga Road lies. Follow the road uphill for several hundred yards and head down Trail #4 when it comes in from the right. Taking this trail downhill can be difficult in poor snow conditions. Be prepared to control your speed from the start. The hill gradually flattens out and the trail drops down into the meadow that the tour started in. Ski straight through to the gas station parking lot. This loop makes a great short tour or a good warm-down at the end of a longer tour.

GIN FLAT LOOP

★★ Quality Rating
■ More Difficult
6.3 miles round trip
Average Skier Time: 4 hours round trip

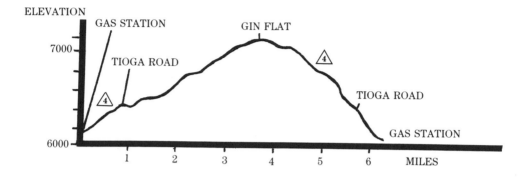

Gin Flat Meadow is a beautiful goal for a ski trip with scenic and varied skiing enroute. The Gin Flat Loop is an excellent hill workout, both going up as well as coming down. Start at the closure gate on the Tioga Road, or from the gas station, via Trail #2. Trail #2 leaves from the middle of the meadow next to the gas station and intersects Trail #4, which can be taken to the Tioga road after one mile. Or, reach this point from the closed Tioga Road trailhead by skiing up the road. Here, the Tioga Road continues up and snakes around an open ridge, with good views to the southwest on clear days. Pass an old controlled burn area on the left. Gradually the road levels out, at a point just over three miles from the start. Here you'll find Gin Flat Meadow and the Tamarack Campground Road on the right. (The campground road is almost two miles long and winds down to dead end at a trailhead that leads to the summit of El Capitan.) To the left is the Old Big Oak Flat Road, labeled as Trail #4, which is the return route for this touring loop and a downhill run that you'll long remember.The old road is not maintained, is narrower than the Tioga Road, and has a few good dips and bumps to negotiate, all of which should keep your attention. If that's not enough, the tight turns will surely test your turning skills. The old road returns you to the junction of Trail #4 on the Tioga Road. You can cross the Tioga Road, and finish on Trail #2, or ski all the way down the road to the closure gate. Of course, for an easier descent from Gin Flat, simply ski back down the way you went up.

CRANE FLAT LOOKOUT

★★★ **Quality Rating**
■ **More Difficult**
2 miles each way
Average Skier Time: 4.5 hour round trip

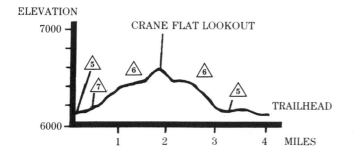

Located on a knob overlooking a large segment of Yosemite National Park, this fire lookout station is manned in the summer and fall months. The views are perfect for spotting fires around the area. When the Park is blanketed with snow each winter and thus without danger of fire, the lookout becomes an exquisite goal for a four mile ski tour. In addition, several possible variations are possible.

To make the most of this tour use trails #5, #6 and #7. From the main trailhead, located just before the closure gate on the Tioga road, use Trail #5, that leads along a mostly flat path for almost half a mile. Turn uphill onto Trail #7 and follow up this steep path for about half a mile before connecting to Trail #6. It is mostly uphill from here to the top.

The views from the lookout are fabulous. Many crests and ranges can be seen in a 360 degree panorama. The return run is a blast. Whether you tuck the entire run without falling, or make a sitzmark every hundred feet, it is still a great, challenging run.Ski back down Trail #6, keeping an eye left for Trail #7. This steep shortcut back to Trail #5 is an exciting downhill section that is worth going back for again and again. Turn left at the bottom of #7 on to #5 and head back to the trailhead.

Skiing Trail #6 (the summer road) from Highway 120 is a more direct route to the lookout and a sensible alternative route. If finding available parking is a problem at the main trailhead, the east end of Trail #5 leads from the gas station to Trails #7, #6 and the top.

CLARK RANGE VISTA

★★ Quality Rating
● Easiest
3 miles round trip
Average Skier Time: 2.5 hours round trip

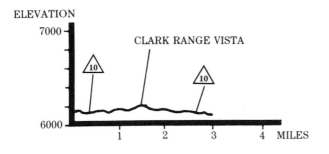

The Clark Range Vista Trail has consistently friendly beginner and inter-
mediate terrain, and interesting views of the Clark Range and Merced
Canyon. Pick up Trail #8, just off Highway 120 at the Crane Flat
Campground Road, usually closed, or Trail #9, across from the gas station.
Trail #8 goes slightly downhill from Highway 120, and follows a series of
small meadows up to join Trail #9 after about ½ mile. If the campground
road is open, you can drive to the end of the road and the beginning of
Trail #10, avoiding Trails 8 and 9 altogether. In any case, follow Trail #10,
winding up and away from the campground, passing through large incense
cedar trees, oaks, manzanita, and alder. Ski to the end of the trail to enjoy
the view before turning to ski back. This trail ends on a ridge that is
somewhat open, and a windbreaker would be a good item to have along
on this tour.

SOUTH LANDING ROAD

★   **Quality Rating**
●   **Easiest**
3 miles round trip
Average Skier Time: 2.5 hours round trip

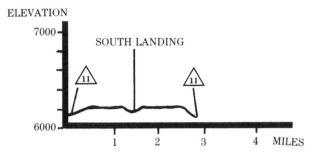

The South Landing Road is across from the main Crane Flat Lookout Road (Trail #6) on Highway 120 west. It follows a gentle path which leads away from all of the other trails in the area, and that in itself is a bonus. Ski past the closure gate and follow the roadbed, winding along a fairly level course that heads southwest. The South Landing Road is very similar to the Clark Range Vista Trail, but ends in an old quarry pit that is used in the summer by Park rangers as a firing range. In the winter, the quarry makes a good training ground for skiers. There is plenty of room to set your own loop for fast track skiing, and plenty of downhill practice runs are also available for skiers of all abilities. On clear days the twin peaks of Mt. Diablo, near San Francisco, can be seen off in the distance to the west, as well as most of the coastal range.

TUOLUMNE MEADOWS AREA

To some people, visiting Tuolumne in the winter is even more appealing than during the rest of the year. The road from the town of Lee Vining, on the east side of the Park, is closed for the sixty miles west to Crane Flat and Tuolumne Meadows is left alone with winter snows. For the winter visitor, there are no crowds to deal with, and a blanket of snow protects the fragile landscape underfoot. Ski touring to Tuolumne in winter is a serious undertaking and plenty of time should be given to preparing and planning for the trip. Blisters, frostnipped feet, altitude sickness, and hypothermia can all become serious problems for the unprepared or inexperienced. Safe passage through avalanche country requires knowledge not encountered on most simpler undertakings. With the right equipment and winter backcountry skills, a trip to Tuolumne Meadows can be a great experience.

Most people ski to Tuolumne by way of the Snow Creek Trail from Yosemite Valley and on to the meadows via Tioga Road. This is usually the easiest route to Tuolumne and can require at least two days of skiing to complete. Others start from Highway 395 at the town of Lee Vining, on the eastern slope of the Sierra. After hiking up to snow line, ski up the grade towards Tioga Pass. The grade is steep, with the trip to the 10,000 foot Tioga Pass requiring a gain of about 3600 feet in twelve miles. From the pass it is another eight miles of mostly downhill skiing to Tuolumne Meadows. This is a somewhat shorter route to the Meadows, but can seem more difficult than a western approach due to the more extreme avalanche danger. The Tioga Road from Crane Flat to Tuolumne is a long thirty-nine mile trek, but it doesn't get skied frequently from Crane Flat to the Snow Creek Trail junction. Don't expect to see many, if any, people on that particular stretch of road.

Many winter travelers to Tuolumne Meadows stay at the "old" visitor center, located just off the main road on the west side of the Tuolumne River bridge. There are electric lights, a woodburning stove and bunkbeds, available on a first-come-first-served basis. Some winter visitors to Tuolumne stay up to two weeks, which is maximum time given on a wilderness permit in the Park. This helps cut down on the impact created by growing numbers of skiers in the backcountry. At times the old visitor center bunks are full so don't count on there being an open bunk. Snow camping is the alternative. One of the warmer areas to make camp is across the meadow, near Soda Springs. That part of the meadow gets the morning sun first, and gets more prolonged sun throughout the day. There are park rangers stationed during the winter near the Tuolumne summer lodge, about one mile east from the old visitor center. They maintain the hut, patrol the area, record snow and weather data, and are happy to assist skiers with questions. It is recommended that you check in with them upon your arrival. As a somewhat bizarre feature to the otherwise wild atmosphere, there are pay phones located outside of the visitor center. They do not require change to reach the operator.

Most of the tours described for the Tuolumne area are fairly long and usually difficult. They assume a base camp in the Meadows area. Know your limits. Before heading out on longer tours, make sure that you can do shorter ones, for your own safety and peace of mind. It is not a bad idea to carry enough equipment to survive an unscheduled bivouac, just in case something goes wrong.

On a trip to Tuolumne you will probably see signs of avalanches along the way. A couple of the spots to watch for avalanches are along the Tioga road from Olmstead Point to the east side of Pywiack Dome and along the high open areas by Tioga Pass. At the west end of Tuolumne Meadows, where the road drops down before Marmot Dome small, but serious slab avalanches sometimes cut loose. Here they have been known to travel through the trees, across the road and into the meadow. It is a good practice to use an avalanche cord (or electronic avalanche beeper) when you encounter an uncertain avalanche situation.U.S.G.S. maps and a compass should be used when there is a question about route finding.

Having plenty of food and water along is important for fighting fatigue and hypothermia. Temperatures in Tuolumne can vary greatly during the winter and it is not uncommon for temperatures to remain well below freezing for weeks at a time. Cold can make snow camping a real chore.

Whether you are snow camping your way to Lee Vining or Mammoth Lakes, or just staying at the visitor center for a few days, you're sure to enjoy your stay in this high country atmosphere. Just be ready for what ever Mother Nature may have in store for you.

Mt. Watkins and Cloud's Rest from the Snow Creek switchbacks

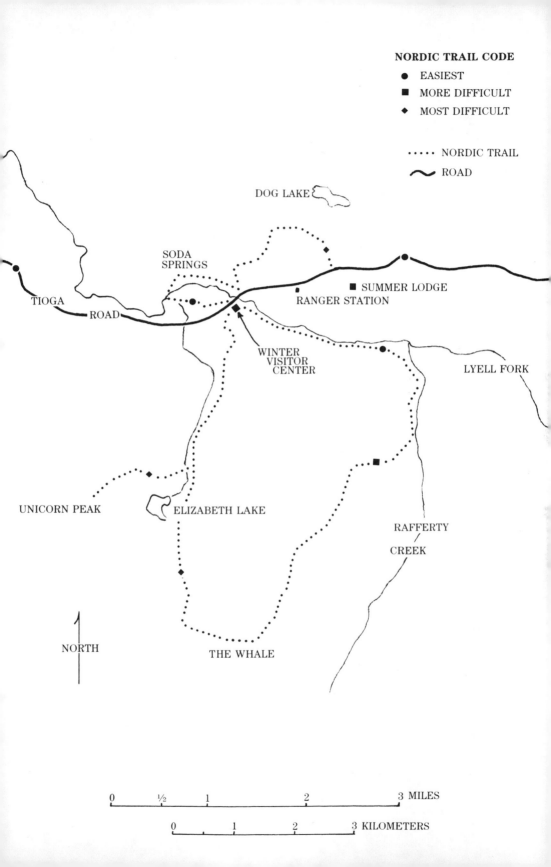

CONTOUR INTERVAL 80 FEET

UNICORN PEAK

★★★   **Quality Rating**
◆   **Most Difficult**
4.2 miles each way
Average Skier Time: 5 hours round trip

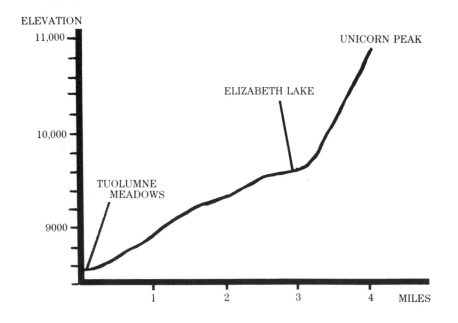

Begin this tour at the start of the summer trail to Elizabeth Lake in the Tuolumne Meadows campground, a short distance west of, and behind, the old visitor center. The start of this trail is in the upper part of the campground, just across from the highest restroom building. Blazes on trees along the trail may or may not be snowed under, but keep an eye out for them, and keep a map and compass handy. Follow the trail as much as possible for about two miles, through sections of deep forest.Veer right and cross Unicorn Creek just before Elizabeth Lake. The peak should be in plain view from here. Switching back and forth, climb onto the open face of the peak and gain elevation to near the saddle between the peak's two summits. The east peak of Unicorn is called Mt. Altusky by local skiers. It is an easy hike to its summit. The "unicorn's horn" is a fairly exposed rock hop to the summit, and is not recommended as a safe winter climb for the novice.

The best line to ski down is usually from the saddle, which is also an excellent spot for lunch and picture taking. The view is spectacular. Open slopes and the altitude combine to give the visitor a very alpine sensation. The ski down is exciting. Be aware of serious avalanche danger from the saddle east toward the lake. In powder, or spring corn conditions, you'll be pleased with this run if your downhill skiing is up to par. If not you may find yourself eating more snow than you ski. Once off the face of Unicorn, the tree skiing back to the campground awaits you. Taking off your ski pole straps here is a good idea. At this point don't risk a dislocated arm or shoulder, because your ski pole hung up in a tree branch. Follow the route that you took up, or forge your way down through the trees back to the Tioga Road.

Skier on Mt. Hoffman   *photo by Chris Cox*

PARSON'S LODGE AND SODA SPRINGS

★ **Quality Rating**
● **Easiest**
2 miles round trip
Average skier time: 2.5 hours round trip

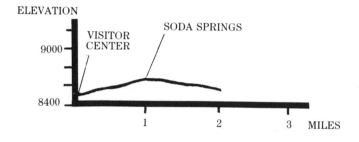

The Soda Springs/Parson's Lodge tour is a good one to save for a stormy day. It is a short distance from the winter visitor center to the Soda Springs area and return. Start by skiing across snow-laden Tuolumne Meadows, veering left and crossing the footbridge over the Tuolumne River. At times Soda Springs can be hard to find, partially obscured by snow. A word of caution: the water is untested and can make one's stomach a little queasy. Parson's Lodge is nearby and although not open in the winter, it is good for composing interesting photographs. A loop can be skied from Parson's Lodge back toward Lembert Dome and the Tioga Road, across the bridge and back to the visitor center. This is a good, short tour, suitable for an easy rest day. Proper sanitation in this area is especially important and outhouses in the area should be used to avoid contaminating the water.

DOG DOME LOOP

★★★   Quality Rating
♦   Most Difficult
3.2 miles round trip
Average Skier Time: 5 hours round trip

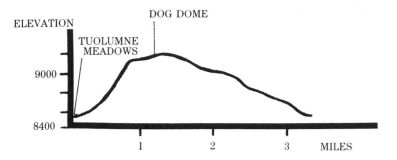

Begin the Dog Dome Loop Trail from the winter visitor center and follow the Tioga Road east, crossing the river just before Lembert Dome. Turn left in front of Lembert Dome and ascend the hill around to the north of the dome.Continue climbing up and right as you pass the dome. Dog Dome comes into view on the right after passing Lembert. The best way to the top of Dog Dome varies with snow depth, so "scope out" the route to the top as you see fit. Although Dog Dome isn't a lofty peak, it offers a nice 360 degree panoramic view. Below you to the southwest is a 200 foot sheer cliff, but the skiable southeast slope is gradual at first. As it descends into the woods it steepens and drops to the Tioga Road, making a great tree run. Ski back either on the Tioga Road, or continue straight, crossing the road and continuing 200 yards to the summer Tuolumne Lodge Road. Take a right on this road to head back to the visitor center, passing the winter ranger residence on the right. From here, keep paralleling the Tioga Road another ½ mile back to the visitor center. Although this is not a long tour, it has a stiff elevation gain of 600 feet to the top of Dog Dome.

ELIZABETH LAKE, THE WHALE, RAFFERTY CREEK LOOP

★★★ **Quality Rating**
♦ **Most Difficult**
12 **miles round trip**
Average Skier Time: 7 hours round trip

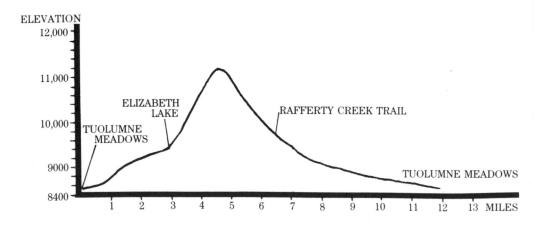

Ski the Elizabeth Lake Trail to Elizabeth Lake as for the tour to Unicorn Peak. Continue around the left side of the lake. The long, ridged peak seen above is known to some as The Whale. Follow up the obvious drainage to the "whale's back". During times of high avalanche danger, this section can be treacherous. Be prepared to abandon the tour if avalanche conditions seem unstable. Follow the ridge up and over the summit. Beware of cornice buildup here, taking care not to get too close to the edge—in places it is very narrow. Drop down the east ridge, winding down and around to the left. Johnson Peak, now to the left, is also an excellent mountain to ski. Scope out the Rafferty Creek drainage while high enough to get a good view of the best way down through the trees to the Rafferty Creek Trail. You will wind up at the head of Lyell Canyon and the Lyell Fork. From here it is a short ski back to the visitor center along the Lyell Fork of the river.

MAMMOTH PEAK

★★★ **Quality Rating**
◆ **Most Difficult**
16 miles round trip
Average Skier Time: 10 hours round trip

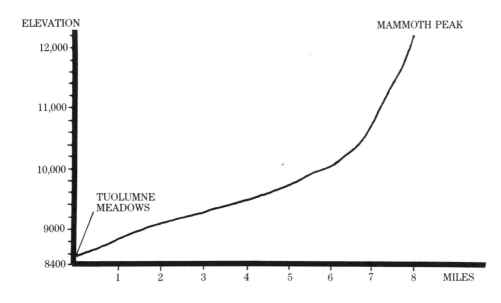

Mammoth Peak, not to be confused with Mammoth Mountain Ski area, is a difficult but exciting peak to bag. Beginning from the Tuolumne Meadows winter visitor center, ski east on the Tioga Road for approximately 4½ miles. With Mammoth Peak on the right, cross over the Dana Fork of the Tuolumne River and head for the far right hand (southwest) ridge of the peak. Ski across the partially wooded meadow, and up through some steep wooded hills before reaching timberline. Once above timberline, attain the open ridge, just before the main summit ridge. Here there is a somewhat flat area that is a good spot to rest before hiking or skiing up the steep summit ridge. Once on the top, take a look down the open bowls of the northeast face, the descent route. This summit area is famous for its cold, high winds, so it is not a great place for a picnic. On the descent, ski down the northeast face to the left, avoiding cliff bands on the right. In places it is steep, so beware of avalanche danger. Continue skiing down and left, skiing into the Parker Creek drainage.The view of the Kuna Crest stretching eastward is incredible, with large frozen high lakes perched below the rocky faces. Ski back toward the Tioga Road via Parker Creek. Once back on the road, it is mostly downhill back to the visitor center.

MT. LYELL

★★★ **Quality Rating**
◆ **Most Difficult**
28 miles round trip
Average Skier Time: 2 days

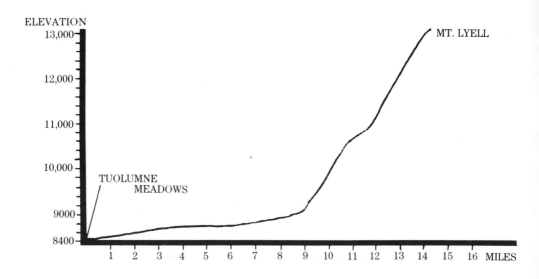

Mt. Lyell, at 13,114 feet in elevation, is the highest peak in Yosemite National Park. Skiing to the top in winter is a serious undertaking. Start from the winter visitor center and take the gentle ski up the Lyell Fork of the Tuolumne River. The John Muir Trail runs through this beautiful V-shaped canyon for about twelve miles to Donohue Pass. After about 9½ miles up the canyon, a short but steep hill will be encountered. Watch for avalanche danger here. Ascend the hill and cross the Lyell Fork. Ski up the left side of the river for approximately another 1½ miles. From here Donohue Pass is to the left and Mt Lyell is another two miles to the right. Ski up a series of rises, with the crest now on your left. There are flat areas here that make good campsites. Continue gaining elevation to where there is a splendid view of Mt. Lyell and Mt. Maclure. Ascend the right hand ridge on Mt. Lyell. Ski down the peak the way that suits your ability. Don't risk problems at this point. Ski back to your basecamp, and cook yourself a well-deserved dinner. The ski back down the canyon to Tuolumne Meadows will seem like a piece of cake after skiing such a peak.

MONO-PARKER PASS AREA

★★★ Quality Rating
♦ Most Difficult
21 miles round trip
Average Skier Time: 10 hours round trip

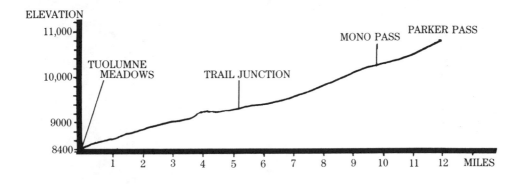

Leave the Tioga Road at the Mono-Parker Pass trailhead, six miles east
from the winter visitor center. Most of the trail signs and blazes will .be
covered with snow, but there are "T" blazes on the trees to help you find
the way. Ski along Parker Creek, eventually traversing up to the ridge on
the left. The views up the canyon are astounding. You are surrounded by
11-13,000 foot high peaks, and the avalanche danger can be high. Now on
the slopes of Mt. Gibbs, traverse higher, heading for Mono Pass. Old,
collapsed cabins, once used by sheep herders can be seen on the west
side of the pass, give the area a lonesome and eerie feeling. Bloody Canyon
and Sardine Lakes lie on the east side of the pass. Years ago, Mono Pass
was a popular Indian crossing to the eastern slopes of the Sierra.Leaving
Mono Pass, climb over the obvious hump on the right and drop down into
Parker Creek, without skiing all the way to Parker Pass. From here it is
an easy ski down the canyon. Pick up your tracks lower down and follow
them back to the Tioga Road and the visitor center.

Backcountry telemarker   *photo by Chris Cox*

MT. DANA FROM TIOGA PASS

★★★ **Quality Rating**
♦ **Most Difficult**
4 miles round trip
Average Skier Time: 3 hours round trip

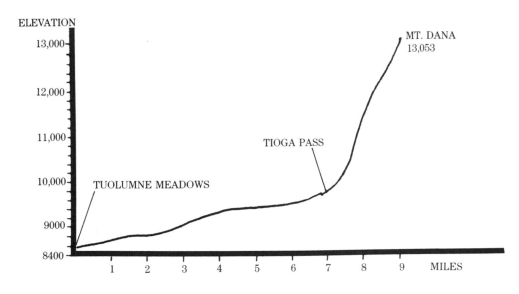

Mt. Dana is one of the highest peaks in the Park, and is easily accessible from Tioga Pass. The best time to ski Mt. Dana is when the pass road is opened early in the spring. At that time of year avalanche danger is low, the snow is "corned up", and many skiers come to hike and ski this 13,053 foot peak. From Tioga Pass ski or hike up the summer trail, marked by rock cairns and blazes on trees. (You will probably see tracks of other skiers.) While some people prefer hiking up, others will ski, using climbing skins or waxes. You will pass to the right of the "Lying Head", an impressive outcropping of rotten rock that faces west. Above, attain the long ridge that leads to the summit. Go up as far as you feel comfortable before pointing the skis back down the hill. Once on the descent, beware of exposed rocks. The amount of time spent hiking or skiing up this peak is well worthwhile. A grand panorama is seen from the summit ridge. Mono Lake, one of the largest saltwater lake in California, and one of the largest rookeries for California sea gulls, may be seen to the east. To the south is the crest of the Sierra Nevada, stretching toward Mammoth Lakes.The northern crest is viewed rising to Matterhorn Peak, near the town of Bridgeport. Nearer peaks and plateaus appear strikingly close, with the frozen lakes below looking like a large string of pearls. All of this adds up to a rigorous and breathtaking high country ski trip.

SCALE 1:62 500

CONTOUR INTERVAL 80 FEET

MT. HOFFMAN FROM YOSEMITE VALLEY

★★★ **Quality Rating**
◆ **Most Difficult**
14 miles each way
Average Skier Time: two days each way

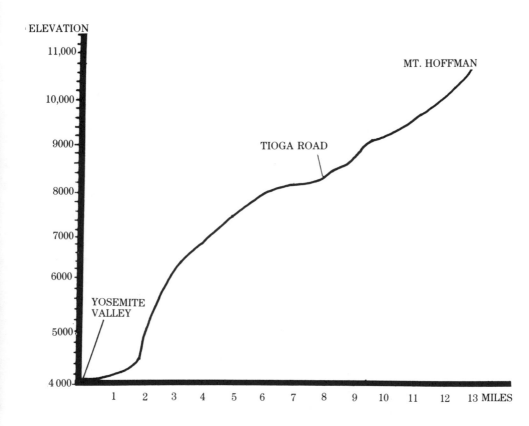

The closest and best way to ski Mt. Hoffman is via the Snow Creek Trail from Yosemite Valley. After about eight miles of hiking and skiing from the Valley, you will arrive at the Snow Creek Trail-Tioga Pass Road junction. See page 60 for more detail in getting to this popular camping spot.

Take time to get a good look at the peak. Check for fresh avalanches, and get an idea of the elevation that you will be gaining. From this junction, cross the road and follow the trail to where it intersects the May

Lake Road. A map and compass may be needed in this area. Get a compass bearing on the peak, look at it on the map, and go for the easiest way up. There are several different possibilities for routes up the face of the peak to the summit. Once again, look for the safest route, avoiding cornices and avalanche zones.This summit has perhaps the best panorama in the Park.Peaks are visible in every direction. Valleys and lakes, and even the distant Illilouette Falls may be seen. The view looking down the slope is also exciting, particularly since you are about to ski it. This descent is definitely steep in places, and hopefully your downhill technique is up to par. Beware of the hazards exposed rocks, trees, and cliff bands may pose. Once at the bottom, as you marvel at your tracks, wishing you had it in you for another run, it is easy to think about all of the other peaks in Yosemite that are still left to bag.

Snow camping below Mt. Hoffman   *photo by Chris Cox*

TRANS-SIERRA TOURS

YOSEMITE VALLEY TO LEE VINING

★★★ **Quality Rating**
♦ **Most Difficult**
40 miles one way
Average Skier Time: 3½ days one way

An early morning start is a good idea for this tour. The Snow Creek switchbacks (105 in all), are a steep, but commonly used way out of Yosemite Valley. South facing, they rarely hold snow very long, and morning hours provide cooler hiking temperatures. Even on a cool day you will probably work up a sweat going up this monstrous trail.

From the top of the switchbacks, ski or hike over easier terrain, following the yellow survey markers on the trees. Cross the Snow Creek Bridge, following a traverse up through thick areas of timber. Pass a couple of smaller streams that cross the trail, and continue following the markers to a small clearing, and a small band of rocks on the left. After this section, climb yet another hill, which levels off before the next hill has to be climbed. The skiing is somewhat easier now, on rolling terrain, with views to the southwest of Cloud's Rest and Half Dome. It's a short distance from here to the Tioga Road. Just before the road you will pass an old snow-covered quarry. The views increase as you get closer to the road, with Mt. Hoffman straight ahead. The trail drops down through the trees and empties out onto the road. If conditions are "fast", good time can be made on this hilly, winding, snow-covered road. Many good campsites can be found from the Snow Creek Bridge to the Tioga Road, as well as along the road itself.

Olmstead Point, just before dropping down to Tenaya Lake, can be a serious avalanche hazard area. Skiing down below the point into the trees is one way to avoid this potentially dangerous area. Tenaya Lake is an excellent choice for camping, skiing, or a rest stop along the way. In the winter the lake is completely frozen, and it is often faster to ski than the road. The peaks and domes in this region often cut loose with spectacular avalanches, so have your camera ready. Leaving the lake, ski uphill along the road to the next avalanche zone, near Pywiack Dome, just off the road to the right. If it appears that the slope might slide, then wait it out—days if necessary—until it is more stable. If it appears stable, make as fast a time as possible while crossing this area. Gaining the experience to adequately judge avalanche conditions takes time. The book by LaChapelle, listed in the appendix, is recommended reading.

Now you are on mostly flat to rolling terrain, winding your way along the road on your way to Tuolumne Meadows. The last big hill before Tuolumne lies between Daff Dome and Fairview Dome. It is a killer, long uphill grade, so don't knock yourself out on the first part. Once at the top of the hill it's all down to the meadows.Watch again for signs of avalanches coming off Marmot Dome, on the right, just before dropping into the meadow.

Leaving the splendor of Tuolumne is difficult but the skiing that awaits is wonderful. "Uphill" is the word that describes the eight miles to Tioga Pass. Some flat easy sections are encountered, with astounding views of neighboring peaks and valleys. Avalanche danger can also be high one mile west of Tioga Pass when the ridge to the left is loaded with snow. The elevation change between Tuolumne and Tioga is about 1300 feet, but once you are there it's all downhill to Lee Vining. You may be faced with serious avalanche danger shortly after leaving the Pass. An early morning start on this section is a good idea. The snow is much more stable during the early morning hours, before the sun has had a chance to loosen it up. From the pass to Lee Vining is 12½ miles, but you will be surprised at how fast it can go under good conditions. Sheer dropoffs into Lee Vining Canyon will certainly keep your attention in this area. Safety should come first here. Once in the lower section of the canyon, there may be minimal snow cover, and it could be necessary to walk. Walking will probably be quite welcome to you after several days on skis, so enjoy this last section, passing the National Forest Ranger station on the right. Behind now are the miles that you've skied, with jagged, snow covered peaks that rise up as if to wave goodbye. For this tour, refer to U.S.G.S. maps Hetch Hetchy Reservoir, Tuolumne Meadows, and Mono Craters.

CRANE FLAT TO LEE VINING VIA TIOGA ROAD

★★★ **Quality Rating**
◆ **Most Difficult**
60 miles one way
Average Skier Time: 4 days one way

This sixty mile road trip originates at the closure gate on the Tioga Road next to Crane Flat Meadow. From here the road rises and winds up to Gin Flat. The snow covered path continues for the next twenty-seven miles over seldom skied countryside, but is worth exploring. There is some avalanche danger, especially in the zone just west of White Wolf. This area is marked as a danger zone and precautions should be taken. Campsites are numerous along this route. The road pauses over a wide range of terrain changes. Mostly uphill skiing is involved, with some level sections, but there are a few good downhill runs. Much of the skiing is in woods, but the views that come and go look to the southeast and west. Once you reach the Snow Creek Trail junction and Tioga Road, evidence of previous skiers may be more obvious.

The majority of skiers use the Snow Creek Trail as a more direct route to and from Yosemite Valley. From this trail junction ski the Tioga road another few miles to Olmstead Point. Not only are there fine campsites available on the west side of the point, but excellent views of Tenaya Canyon, and the high country. After crossing the avalanche zone at Olmstead Point, continue downhill to Tenaya Lake, where the road levels before turning uphill again. More avalanche evidence can be seen as the road rises between the lake and Pywiack Dome. The skiing gets easier for a time until the last big uphill section is encountered near the base of Daff Dome. This long grind seems to go on forever, but your reward lies just ahead with Tuolumne Meadows spreading out before you like an ocean of snow. Continue on to Lee Vining as for the previous tour. Refer to U.S.G.S. maps Lake Eleanor, Hetch Hetchy Reservoir, Tuolumne Meadows, and Mono Craters.

YOSEMITE VALLEY TO MAMMOTH VIA TUOLUMNE MEADOWS

★★★ **Quality Rating**
◆ **Most Difficult**
63 miles one way
Average Skier Time: 4 days one way

Every winter and spring experienced cross-country skiers come from afar to begin a classic trans-Sierra tour to the town of Mammoth Lakes.Originating at the Snow Creek Trail near Mirror Lake, proceed up the switchbacks to the valley rim and continue on to Tuolumne Meadows as for the previous tour.

Beyond Tuolumne the going gets tougher and you should be aware of avalanche conditions ahead. Ski up Lyell Canyon, following the Lyell Fork of the Tuolumne River. As you near the upper section of the canyon, avalanche danger increases. The terrain steepens as you ascend through thick forest. Cross the Lyell Fork and ski up the left side of the fork through more open terrain to timberline. The route levels a bit where Donohue Pass becomes visible to the left. Mt. Lyell and Mt. Maclure are up the canyon to the right. Ski up and left to Donohue Pass. In clear weather most of the route ahead is visible. On either side of this 11,000 foot pass views are awesome. Ski down to the left off the pass. Continue over this magnificent back country to Thousand Island Lake. Some choose to camp here for the wild scenery and protection of tree cover. From here Badger Lakes is just ahead, leading to the long San Joaquin Ridge.

This prominent ridge offers a high route to Minaret Road at Minaret Summit. In high avalanche danger the ridge keeps you above most of the avalanche areas that tend to "run" down into lower sections of the canyon. Pass just below San Joaquin Mountain and the Two Teats. Drop down to Deadman Pass and up the other side. From here the ridge snakes down to Minaret Summit and snow covered Minaret Road. Then it's all downhill to Mammoth Mountain Ski Area. Telephones and food are available inside the lodge. Shuttle buses to town are provided at minimal cost. For this tour, refer to U.S.G.S. maps Yosemite Valley, Hetch Hetchy Reservoir, Tuolumne Meadows, Mono Craters, and Devils Postpile.

APPENDIX

Recommended Reading

There are many books available on every aspect of cross country skiing. The following is a partial list.

The A.B.C. of Avalanche Safety, by E.R. LaChapelle, The Mountaineers
Waxing for Cross-Country Skiing, by Michael Brady and Lorns Skemstad, Wilderness Press
Wilderness Medicine, by William Forgey M.D., Indiana Camp Supply Books

Cross Country Ski Gear, by Michael Brady, Mountaineers
The new Complete Snow Campers Guide, by Raymond Bridge, Scribners

Mountain Skiing, by Vic Bein, The Mountaineers
Mountaineering First Aid, by Dick Mitchell, The Mountaineers
Cross-Country Skiing, by Ned Gillette and John Dostal, The Mountaineers

Ski Touring in California, by Dave Beck, Wilderness Press
Be Expert with Map and Compass, by Kjellstrom, Scribners
Backcountry Skiing, by Lito Tejada-Flores, Sierra Club Books

the skier's
ten commandments

carry thy own skis and thy knap-
sack that thy friends shall not
avoid thee, and that thy days
shall be long on the ski trips
that thou makest.

thou shalt not dither.

thou shalt not commit sitzmarks.

thou shalt not swipe thy neighbor's ski wax.

thou shalt not bear false witness
of thy downhill runs, nor thy jump
turns, nor thy telemarks.

thou shalt not covet thy neighbor's

sealskins, nor thy neighbor's agility, nor his stem-christiania, nor his closed-christiania, nor his open-christiania, nor any other christiania which is thy neighbor's.

"sitzmarks are made by fools like me, but only fritsch can miss a tree."

thou shalt have no other sports before ski.

thou shalt not take with thee any toboggans, nor any other means of transportation from the heavens above to the earth beneath.

remember the winter time and keep it wholly; in the summer thou shalt labor and do all thy work, but the winter is the season of the ski, thy lord and master. in it's evenings thou shalt not fritter away thy time with backgammon, nor with red-dog, nor michigan, nor tiddley-winks, nor jigsaw puzzles, but in the sweat of thy brow thou shalt polish and wax thy skis. for in ten hours thou shalt labor and climb up the hill and in ten minutes shalt be down again.

(oh yeah)